MIKE NELSON
TRIPLE BLUFF CANYON

MODERN ART OXFORD 8 May - 4 July 2004
Organised by Modern Art Oxford

Director: Andrew Nairne
Curator: Suzanne Cotter
Assistant Curator: Miria Swain
Programme Administrator: Dawn Scarfe
Gallery Manager: Andrew Paterson
Installation Technicians: Tom Legg, Adam J. Maynard, Justin Neal,
Ruairiadh O'Connell, Rajesh Punj, Stuart Turner, Ben Young
Operations Manager: Jo Raw

Assistants to Mike Nelson: Paul Carter, Ross Taylor, Tom Dale

With special thanks to Brian Aldiss, Sally Craddock, Michael Craven,
Rosalind Horne, Simon Josebury, Robin Klassnik, Rachel Lowe,
Matt's Gallery (London), Jeremy Millar, Jennifer Mojika, Isabel Nelson,
Suzy Prior, Ruth Rattenbury, Phil Smith

TRIPLE BLUFF CANYON HAS BEEN GENEROUSLY
SUPPORTED BY ARTS COUNCIL ENGLAND, SOUTH EAST
AND THE ELEPHANT TRUST

©Modern Art Oxford 2004

Published by Modern Art Oxford
Edited by Suzanne Cotter
Assisted by Miria Swain
Picture Research by Dawn Scarfe
Colour installation photography by John Riddy
(except page 88: Mike Nelson)
Designed by Secondary Modern
Printed by Special Blue in and edition of 1750 copies

ISBN: 1 901 352 20X
Distributed in the UK by Cornerhouse.
70 Oxford Street
Manchester M1 5NH
England
www.cornerhouse.org/publications

Modern Art Oxford
30 Pembroke Street
Oxford OX1 1BP
England
Tel: + 44 (0)1865 722 733
www.modernartoxford.org.uk

The *Enigma of Isidore Ducasse* © Brian Aldiss 2004
Ordo Ob Chao © Jeremy Millar 2004
Isidore, Ink on paper, © Brian Aldiss 2004

Cover image: cover, *Arts Magazine* Special Issue: Robert Smithson,
May 1978 © Estate of Robert Smithson/ VAGA, New York/ DACS,
London, 2004

Unless otherwise mentioned all images are from the collection of
Mike Nelson, with the kind permission of:
Antikvarisk-Topografiska Arkivet (ATA), 38
Bureau of American Ethnology, Smithsonian Institution, 54
Cambridge University Museum of Archaeology and Anthropology
Accession no.P.8941.ACH1, 53
Cambridge University Museum of Archaeology and Anthropology
Accession no. P.8593.ACH1, 42
Janet & Colin Bord, Fortean Picture Library, 31
© The Guardian, Ewen MacAskill (text), Ali Haider/EPA (image), 41
Historisk Museum, Bergen, Norway, 51
Maj Jorgensen, Copenhagen National Museum, 50
Photography Division, Miriam & Iva D. Wallach Division of Art, Print
& Photograph, The New York Public Library, 43
Photography Division, Miriam & Iva D. Wallach Division of Art, Print
& Photograph, The New York Public Library York Public Library,
Astor, Lenox and Tilden Foundations, 44
University of London Library, Harry Price Library [Astrologer], 73, 75
H. Roger-Viollet, 71
John Webb, FRPS, 77

Modern Art Oxford is supported by Oxford City Council, Arts Council
England, South East, and the Horace W. Goldsmith Foundation.
Museum of Modern Art. Registered charity no. 313035

supported by

TRIPLE BLUFF CANYON

MIKE NELSON

With a short story by
Brian Aldiss and an essay by
Jeremy Millar

MODERN ART OXFORD

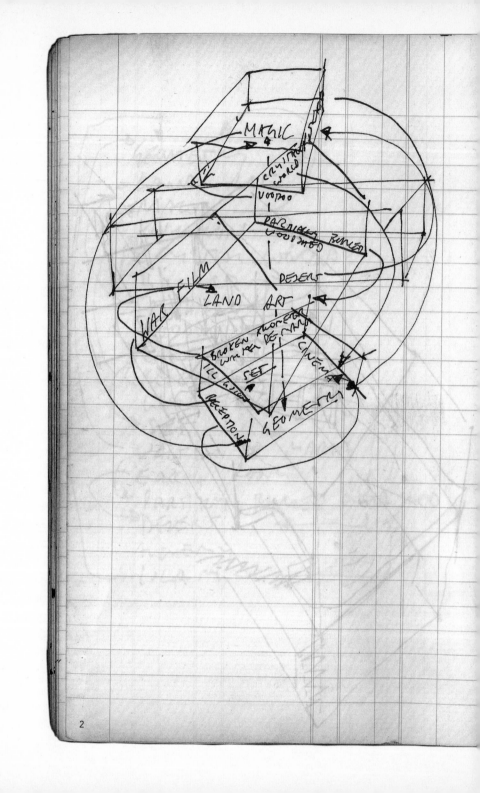

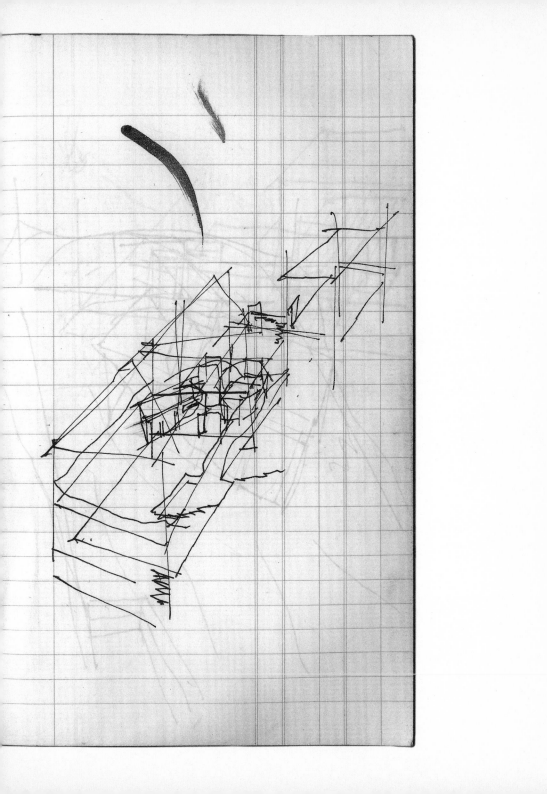

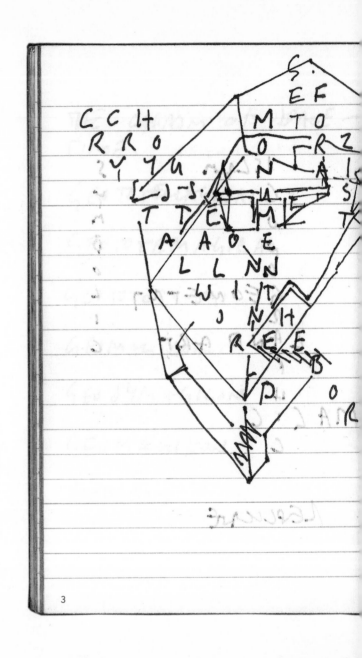

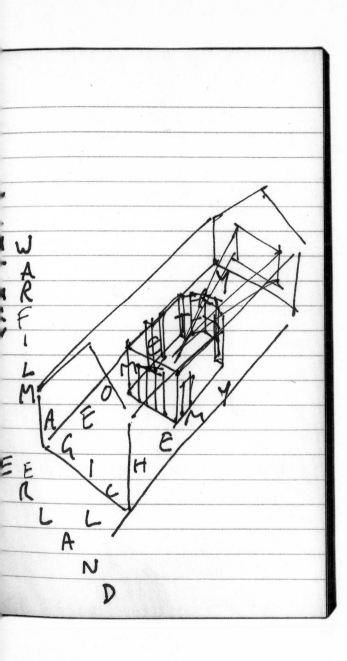

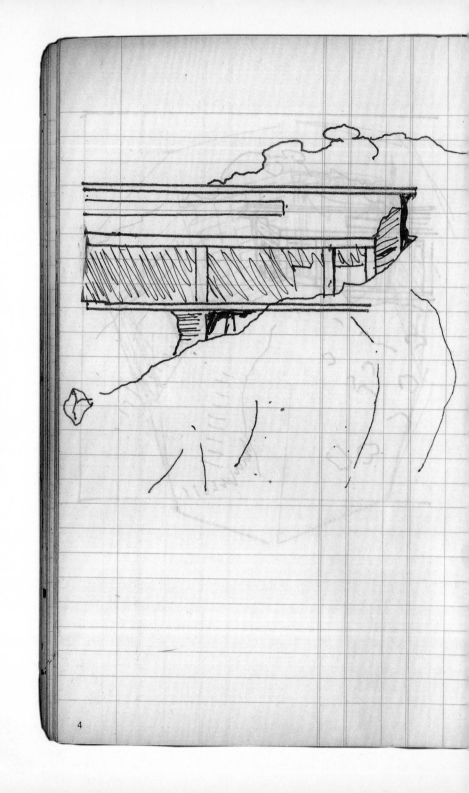

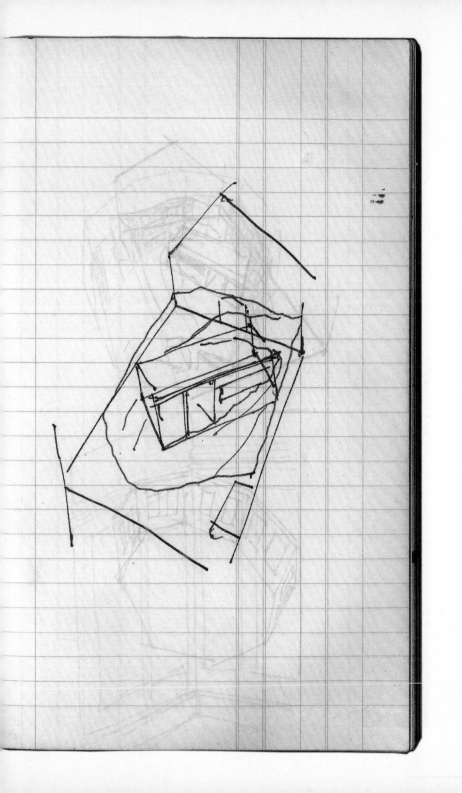

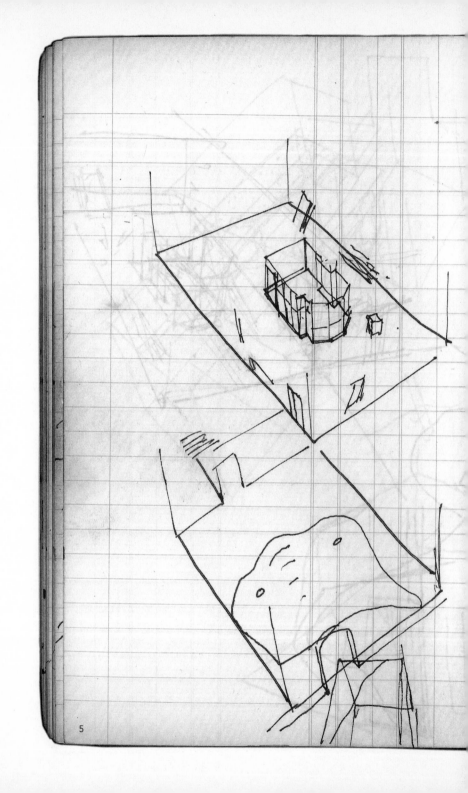

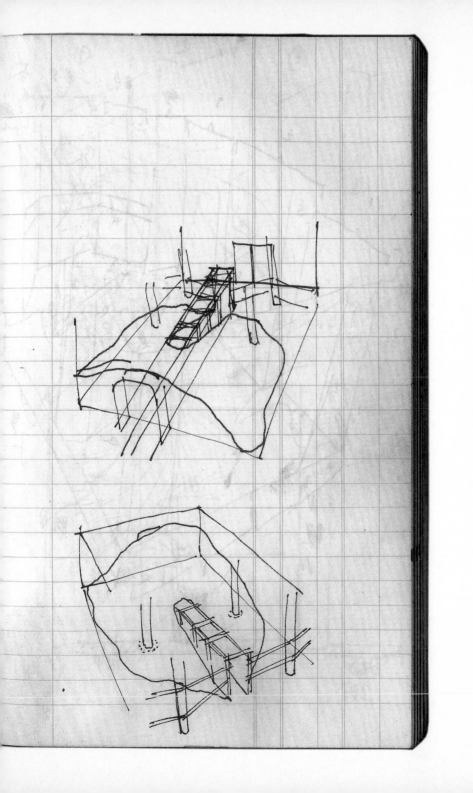

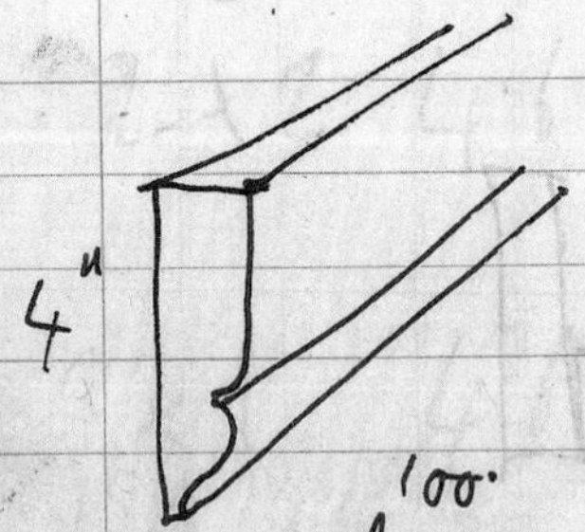

4"

'00'
lever

2ob

4"

2½" screws

THE BROTHERHOOD OF fuerty

al-Jubir (for photo comparis.
in restoration)

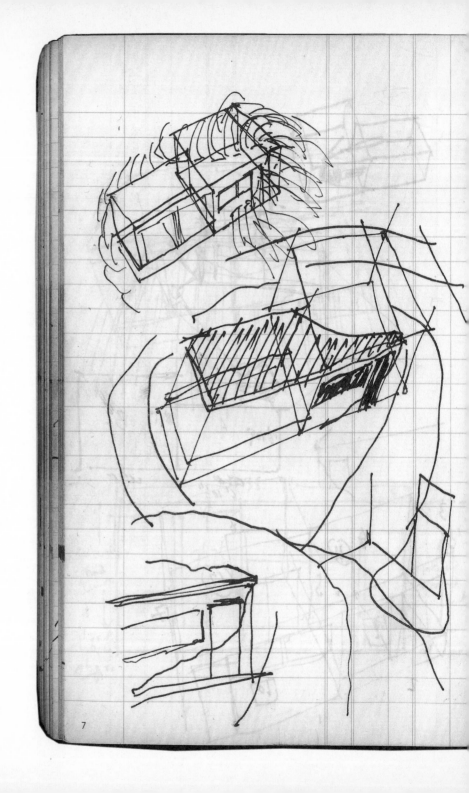

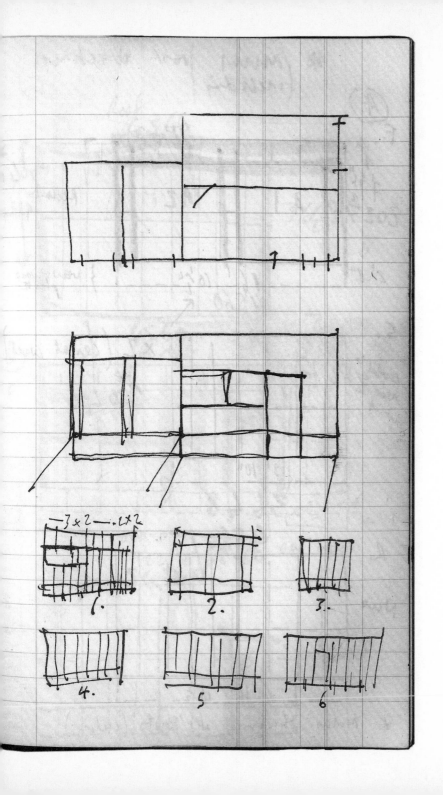

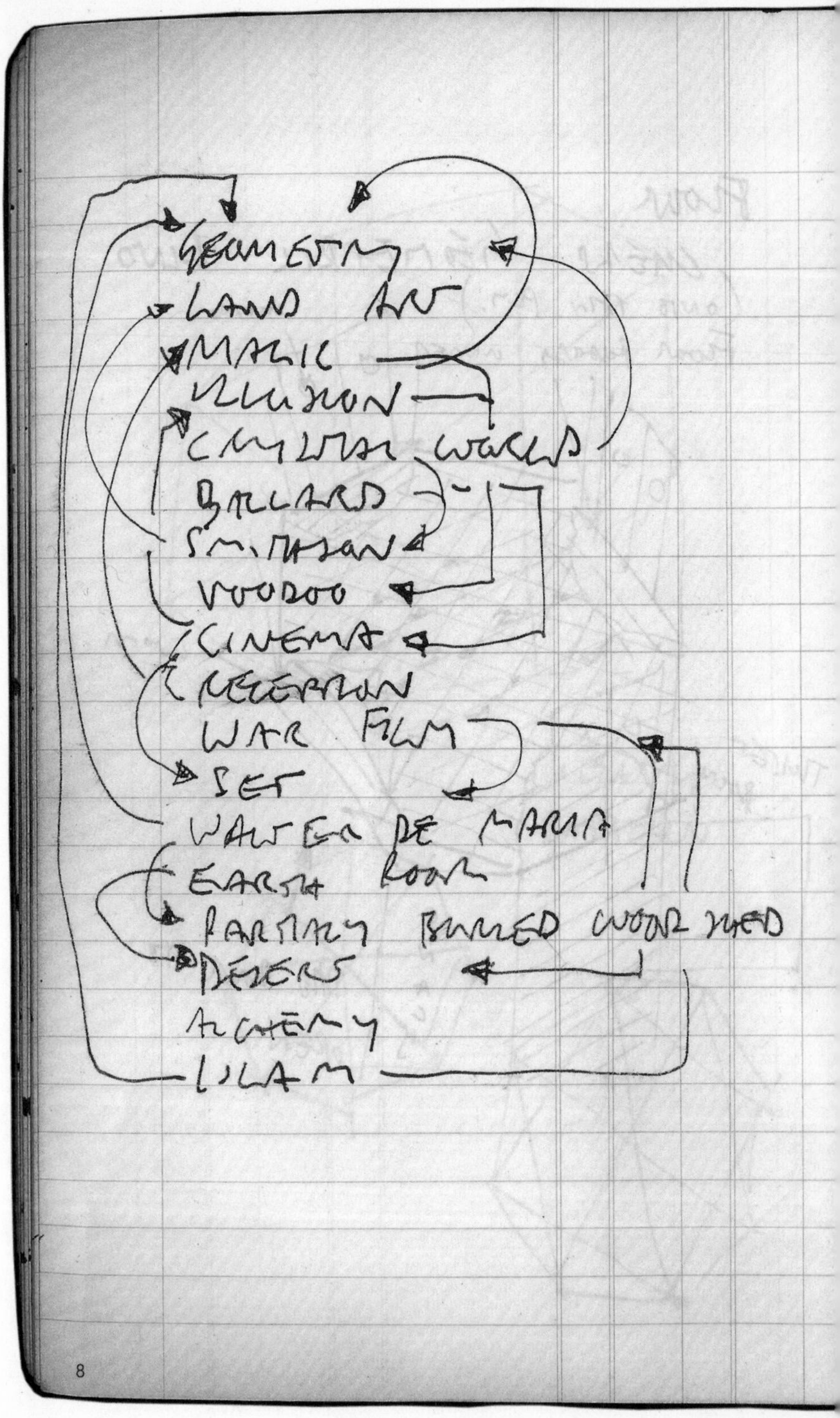

GEOMETRY
LAND ART
MAGIC
ILLUSION
CHILDISH WORLD
BALLARD
SMITHSON
VOODOO
CINEMA
RECEPTION
WAR FILM
SET
WALTER DE MARIA
EARTH ROOM
PARTIALLY BURIED WOODSHED
DESERTS
ALCHEMY
ISLAM

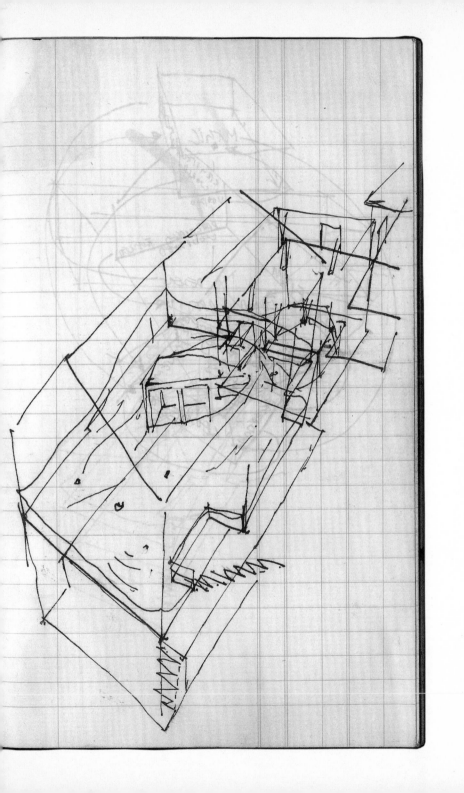

10

11

12

13

15

16

20

THE ENIGMA OF ISIDORE DUCASSE

Brian Aldiss

The fires to keep away dream-killers were still burning. Their flickering glow played against the brutal outline of the ancient casemate which dominated the scene. Stepping through the sheets of smoke, Isidore Ducasse approached her dream home. She had said good-night to Raymond Mann, her mysterious friend. She climbed the dune to where the hut stood, half-buried in sand. Gulls screamed overhead. A flying boat, a recreation of a machine that had existed a century past, flew low overhead, to splash down, neatly as a swan on a still lake, on the North Sea.

Isidore worked like a burrowing animal in order to get to her front door. Every day, the sand proliferated. She squeezed through the doorway and wrenched the door shut behind her. She stood in the hall, not really thinking, listening to the groan of timbers under the increasing weight of artificial landscape.

She never ate at this time of year. The fish had emigrated to the South Atlantic. She put on a CD. Sid Phillips and his Band played 'I've Found a New Baby'; it was the one tune she really enjoyed. Stripping herself naked, she switched on the television. Channel Two was showing Botticelli's painting, *Primavera*. She sat for several minutes, staring at it. The dream figures maintained their pose. The multiplicity of flowers never wilted. Nothing stirred. The house creaked as she watched the picture for signs of movement. It was a beautiful painting, like a drugged dream.

AUTHOR'S NOTE

While I was writing my prose poem, the electricity in my sector of Oxford failed. With a squark, my CD player died. My phone would not work. The heating went. More particularly, my computer gave up the ghost.

The current surged back within twenty minutes. I switched the computer on again. As I feared, my story had vanished, all but the first two paragraphs, which I had saved earlier.

I had to begin my work again. Somewhere in the void, a ghost version of the following exists. The following is itself a ghost version of our lives.

The half-clad figures were emblems of something she could not understand but liked nevertheless. Finally, she switched off and went to lie on her couch. The ancient joints of the hut creaked as if it was a bygone wooden galleon. The perpetual workings of men had brought the earthworks about her ears. She lay naked between sheet and duvet. Before she switched off the light, she watched a fine light rain of sand grains, in a corner of the room, seeping like a fluid from rafter to floor. She lived in a giant hour-glass. One day, one time, she would be buried alive.

She flipped off the light and the room disappeared. Only the sound of it remained, like an impediment in the blood, like the intimations of tinitus. She reached out in the dark for the little silver box by her bed. From it she extracted a pill and, just as blindly, gulped water from a bottle standing nearby. Isidore curled up on her right side and tucked her hand between her thighs, where no sand penetrated. Her thought was of the great sullen casemate nearby, but it elongated amazingly and turned to the colour of the surrounding sand. And then the operculum opened.

Isidore had to press her way through a thicket of twigs of a species she could not identify. They were caught in the rays of a low-lying sun, so that she moved through a golden maze. The twigs appeared to move out of her way as she approached, as if to protect the infant buds on their stems. The buds were tipped with green. Every now and again as she progressed, a bud would open a misty blue eye, as if making an obscure signal; barely had she glimpsed it than the bud would close again.

Now her naked figure was through the maze, into an area of golden darkness, an alcheringa recalling a dreamed-of past: a past where no work was done, fruit fell from trees and water was always crystal-pure. Bewildered, she was aware of pale feet pattering down a wide staircase. They moved daintily from stone slab to stone slab in hypnotic movement. She realised they were her own feet, in semi-autonomous action. The slabs were of a rock laid down eons ago, in the warm waters of an ocean of the Triassic period, when intelligence had yet to be born. She felt the warmth of the bygone seas. Each stair contained fossils of extinct shrimp-like creatures, which struggled to escape their incarceration in stone and time. In her ear, the sound of their writhings was a faint sea wave. Shhh, shhh...

Her attention was fixed not on the stairs down which she progressed but on the baby she cradled in her arms. The child gazed up into Isidore's face with absolute trust. Its sex was indeterminate. Isidore hugged it and kissed its cheek. Its wide eyes were like a clear blue sky as it smiled a smile of unmitigated happiness. It struck straight to Isidore's emotional centres. By reflex she smiled back into the dear vision of serenity. Mutual happiness was theirs. "This is I as a child," she murmured to herself, "before I encountered the world, the other world..." Pause. "The world of casemates..." Even as she whispered the words to herself, the lovely babe faded. Full of regret, she could only clutch herself

She was forced to concentrate on her descent, and on the cactus-like plants fringing the stairway. Their flat spikey ears were now seen, in a constant mesenchyme of turning and folding, to be not leaves but faces - the faces of a nondescript and hypogeal crowd. As the light grew, as she advanced, she saw there were some persons who wore masks, or at least some whose boney features resembled birds or beaked animals. Some turned towards her, in threat or supplication. They sought her or her blood. Accompanying them was a tantalising pheromone of music, which grew elaborately, as the population thinned, into an oppressive melody. She strove to recognise it.

Now she was able to take in the immensity of the staging through which she passed. It was as though thought itself had an arcane architecture visible to the eye. Its structures billowed on every side. She was now on level ground. The stairs were left behind. Her feet were no longer naked. As she went on her way, elements of her surroundings drifted with her, their antics recalling the gestures of a drugged oriental dancer. A melancholy tune, its theme amplified and often repeated, spoke of a sense of solitude. She was overwhelmed by its chords, from which there seemed no escape. She longed again for the babe that had been.

She quickened her pace. The way became steeper. The music died. Round her lay only a flat plain. It spoke not of desolation but peace. She saw the operculum and floated through it. A brief black panel slid aside.

Isidore was back in her room where the sands of time drifted down like a mist. The grains made a minute sound as they fell. She showered herself. The water ran down her body and disappeared like a silver snake through a small circular grating. She dried herself and powdered herself. She put on rough clothing.

With an effort, she squeezed through the ever-closing door to the outdoor panorama. The dune remained, ever encroaching. There over the artificial landscape loomed the bleak black bulk of the casemate, remaining ruinously indestructable from the earlier hostilities. Two men in overalls stood together on the dune. One said to the other, "He cares a great deal about ecology." The other laughed and said, "Everyone does!"

She walked through them and down into the gallery. She had left the real world behind. Now she was in the world of make-believe.

...mas slogans, West Bank.

Tordai

31

32

35

36

38

39 沙坡头旅游纪念 副券 无副券无效

40

A coalition showing signs of fracture

rategy Insurgents are targeting forces of smaller countries, exposing the weaknesses in the Pentagon's plans

MacAskill Diplomatic editor

he Shia uprising is exposing the fragility of the US-led coalition in Iraq and putting a strain on the smaller partners.

While the 110,000-strong US nd the 8,700-strong British force red for combat, many of the other es joined the coalition in expecta-peacekeeping and reconstruction. e dismay of US central command, se and South Korean forces have ed to their compounds after under fire, while Ukrainian and forces have been driven out of the Kut by Shia fighters. The US mil-considering whether it needs to y 25,000 expected reinforcements s sector around Baghdad to the bolster the coalition forces. The on has already shored up its troop deal with the deepening chaos by the rotation of some 25,000 sol-ue to go home after a year in the e.

reds more British troops flew out yesterday. More than 300 mem-he Princess of Wales's Royal Reg-lus Territorial Army soldiers from sgow-based 52nd Lowland Regi-ft for Basra, where they will form the 4,500-strong 1st Mechanised .

ut the support of either the UN or e US has been unable to call on es such as France, Germany, India stan for troops. Instead it has had on a ragtag coalition of about 40 es as diverse as El Salvador and ia. Between them they contribute troops in non-combat roles, pri-engineering.

rs from Spain, Ukraine, Italy, ador and Poland have come under s week, as well as the Americans kish. One of the first casualties this as a Salvadorean soldier in Najaf. nian soldier was killed on Tuesday A Ukrainian defence official said that his country's troops would e Iraq, but had withdrawn from they are not fit for hostilities". ountry other than Spain has to pull its forces out of Iraq, but vy fighting has caused rethinks in capitals. The chances of these es responding positively to calls troops are fast diminishing.

governments are discussing they will send replacements eir tour of duty ends. Kazkhstan, not intend to replace its 27 oes not intend to replace its 27 rs when its term is up on May 30.

A US marine confronts a relief convoy sent from Baghdad for the residents of Falluja Photograph: Ali Haider/EPA

The partners

United States provides the vast majority of troops with 110,000.
UK contributes 8,700.
Other forces include:
Poland 2,500, **Italy** 2,500, **Singapore** 200, **Czech Republic** 150, **Denmark** 380, **Portugal** 100, **Lithuania** 65, **Norway** 100, **Netherlands** 1,000, **New Zealand** 60, **Australia** 850,

but sending more soldiers was out of the question.

The kidnapping of three Japanese civilians in Iraq added to the pressure on the Tokyo government, which is already facing domestic opposition to its involvement in Iraq. Japan has had a pacifist constitution since the end of the second world war and there is continuing resentment at the decision to send troops.

The Japanese prime minister, Junichiro Koizumi, said yesterday: "It appears that

eney leaves today for a week-long trip to Japan, China and South Korea.

The exploitation of the weaknesses in the coalition does not appear to have been part of a coordinated strategy by the insurgents. The US deliberately placed the weaker coalition forces in the Shia areas of the south and central Iraq, which had been relatively quiet until this week. When the attacks came, the weakness quickly became obvious.

Japan

were carrying guns and about a third of them were wearing masks," Lim Young-sup, a church minister, told Reuters. The seven were blindfolded and taken to a house by the kidnappers, where they were held for five hours before being freed after proving they were not soldiers.

Ukraine

The 1,650-strong detachment suffered its first casualty in Kut on Tuesday, and has since withdrawn from the town. "Despite the difficult situation, the withdrawal of the Ukrainian contingent from Iraq is not on the agenda," Oleh Syvushenko, deputy chief of Ukraine's general staff said. But senior Ukrainian MPs said yesterday that once a "more complete picture" of events in Iraq emerged, the parliament might put forward a motion to withdraw troops.

Kazakhstan

The defence minister said he considered it expedient to withdraw the 27 troops who were recently stationed with the Ukrainians in Kut. "You know that the term of our second group is about to expire. Therefore we have suggested not to send the next contingent to Iraq after the term expires and end the mission there," General Mukhtar Altynbayev said.

Bulgaria

Bulgaria has 480 troops in Iraq assisting the Polish-led force near Kerbala. The defence ministry said their base had come under mortar fire on Tuesday, but there were no casualties. It has declined a request to complement the Polish-led battalion in central-southern Iraq after the anticipated withdrawal of Spanish troops in June.

Australia

The prime minister, John Howard, who has sent 850 military personnel to serve in and around Iraq, is running into fresh trouble because of his pro-US stand. The war is an issue in a federal election due by late this year, with the opposition Labour party advocating bringing troops home by Christmas. The former prime minister Malcolm Fraser compared the situation in Iraq to the Vietnam war. "In both cases, you had a largely American army, not completely but largely, trying to support or establish a state in a country that was foreign and alien to them," he told Australian Broadcasting Corporation radio.

New Zealand

Wellington said it will pull its 60 army engineers out of Iraq in September, though they may return later.

Singapore

of the hostages and vowed to continue its mission in Iraq.

South Korea

South Korea has 600 military engineers and medics in Iraq, who were confined to their bases during the latest spate of fighting. Seoul is looking at the two northern provinces of Irbil and Sulaimaniya for its

47

THE OFFERING—SAN ILDEFONSO

50

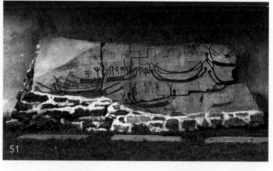

51

53

**SAVE
AMERICA'S
FARMS**

American Farmland Trust

52

54

59

60

61

62

64

LA MAGIA NEGRA

65

66

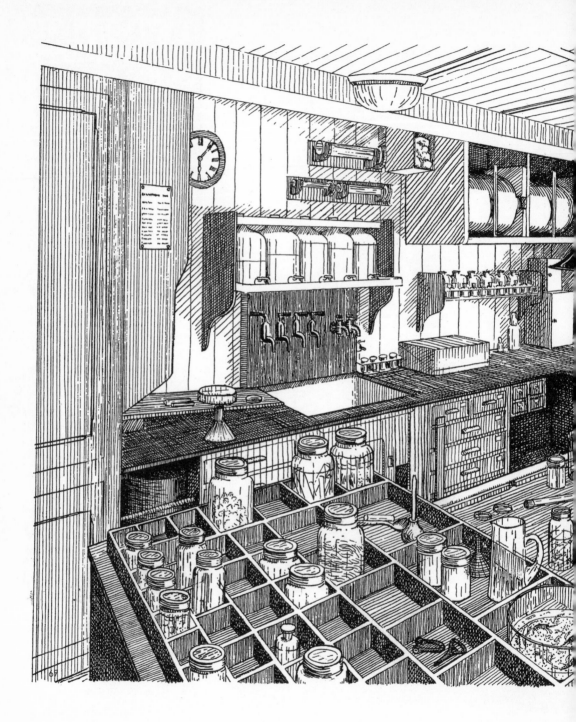

68

69

Magic Ceremonies.

"Such were the mystic rites, ceremonies and incantations, used by the ancient Theurgists to burst asunder the bonds of natural order, and to obtain an awful intercourse with the World of Spirits."

Vide page 227.

LONDON.

Published by William Charlton Wright, 65, Paternoster Row.

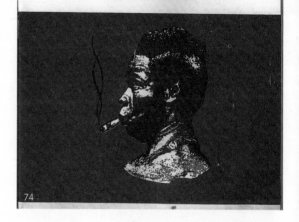

7 POTENCIAS CORTE AFRICANA
VIEJO Y NUEVO
MAGIA NEGRA Y BLANCA

ENCENDEMIENTO DE VELAS
USO DE RAICES Y ACEITES,
POLVOS E INCIENSO
GUIA PARA ESPIRITISTAS
NEDIANTES Y LECTOR

74

The Astrologer
OF THE NINETEENTH CENTURY.

75

CIRCLE THE FIRST.

LOS ADMIRABLES
SECRETOS DE
ALBERTO EL GRANDE

3.00

GRANDES SECRETOS NATURALES
VIRTUDES DE HIERBAS, PIEDRAS Y ANIMALES

76

78

79

80

FREEDOM FESTIVALS and EVENTS

81

HIPPY

al summer problem of
campments on Welsh
l has increased in
s year. An estimated
ellers invaded Bala
d before moving on to
land near Llandrindod
owys, where Welsh
ndent **Robert Davies**
p with them.

community of Llanbister
now how to cope with the
of shabby vehicles that
pearing one evening en
he unfenced common lying
t of the village.
imply locked themselves
hem patrolled hoping to
ft.

with rights on the com-
nded up their flocks to
hem from the travellers'
d farmers throughout the
eased their vigilance. In-
y the growing number of
hey called a public meeting
y were told that the police
werless without a court

hill farmer Eddie Price.
ad as a magistrate for more
ears and is still on the Lord
r's retired list, is con-
at the normal tenets of law
are being destroyed by the
number hippies who have
mid-Wales this summer.

of timber

rveyed the remains of his
ed that was demolished by
ay hippy-owned vehicle.
e, Llwynych, Llanbister,
had no sympathy for the
ellers illegally camped on
y common.
have opted out of all of
responsibilities, but none of
igen," he said. " If, as we

to control this menace, they must be
given them.
"They certainly have authority to
enforce vehicle licensing and road
worthiness laws which are being
blatantly flouted. What has hap-
pened to this tiny rural community
is totally intolerable. People are
afraid to leave their property un-
guarded, livestock is threatened by

the large number of dogs these people insist on keeping, and quiet
county roads have become danger-
ous to use."
Forstry contractor Graham
Parker said he had not been to work
since the hippy invasion as theft was
rife and elderly villagers were terri-
fied, even though extra police had
been stationed in the area.

Hippies camped out on common land. Other likely sites are being sprayed with slurry.

At the vast illegal camp
ellers sheltered from torren
in old buses, ambulance
teepees and caravans, and
just wanted to be left alo
life their way.
A poet called Shed admi
many of them saw land
grasping capitalists tryin
on to land stolen from the
who once worked it. Com
in their view, was our
nation, and they had as m
to use it as chartered grazie

Prejudice allegation

Tony Mensies, who until
ran a hostel for the ho
Kings Cross, blamed ar
with farmers on the sh
approved campsites and
against an alien lifestyle t
ers would never understan
Others claimed that the
would increase as more un
youngster reacted to ch
social services support by
the road and demanding

83

84

85

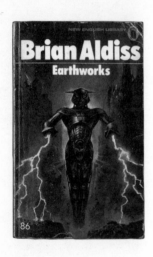

86

87

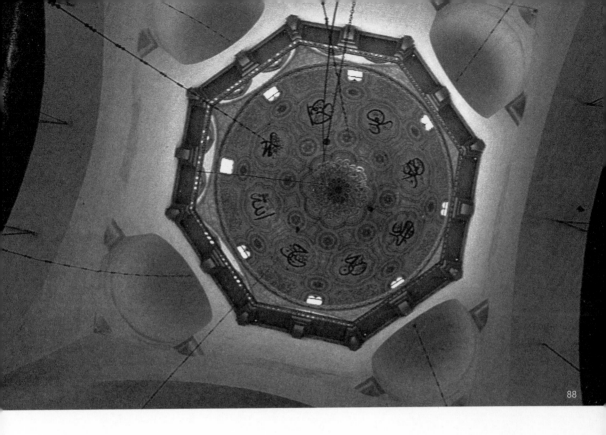

88

89

ORDO AB CHAO

Jeremy Millar

'All that remains of the experience of the temple in the desert is the destitution before the empty temples.'
Jean-Luc Nancy

'The disaster ruins everything, all the while leaving everything intact.'
Maurice Blanchot

It seems that no matter how it ends, it always begins with chaos. One of the earliest extant creation myths, that of the Pelasgian dating from around 3500 B.C., has it that: 'In the beginning, Euronyme, the Goddess of All Things, rose naked from Chaos, but found nothing substantial for her feet to rest upon, and therefore divided the sea from the sky, dancing lonely upon its waves.' In Hesiod's *Theogony* also, written in the seventh century B.C. we learn that 'Verily first of all did Chaos come into being, and then broad-bosomed Gaia, a firm seat of all things forever…' The Ainu people of Japan believed that 'In the beginning the world was slush, for the waters and the mud were all stirred together', while according to a southern Chinese myth, the creator god P'an Ku chiselled the land and sea apart. We will perhaps recall a more familiar account in Genesis, in which a similar act of separation takes place between sea and earth, when God commands, 'Let the waters under the heavens be gathered together into one place, and let the dry land appear.' Of course, this is not the first act of creation — God had already created the heavens and the earth, even if the earth was at this stage 'without form and void, and darkness was upon the face of the deep' — but rather an act of differentiation, the shaping of material *already there* rather than an act of creation *ex nihilo*.

In none of these myths (and there are plenty more which share their characteristics) do we find that the earth, seas or heavens were created nowhere and out of nothing. Not only are such concepts impossible to conceptualise — simply, how would one describe absolute nothingness? — but as such they would also create great difficulties in imagining a shift from this radical nothingness into the beginnings of the world that we see around us. Consequently, what we find is not the absolute void, but rather what we might call a relative void, a region of shapelessness and indeterminacy, a 'substantial nothingness' known as chaos. This is not chaos as we might now consider it, however, as a scene of disorder or confusion, but rather a scene of emerging order, an opening — as in *chasm*, with which it shares a Greek root — in which things might come into being. As the philosopher Edward S. Casey has remarked in considering these issues:

> The ancient notion of chaos as a primal abyss or gap points in this same direction: a gap is both an opening *between* two already existing things (e.g., earth and sky) and an *opening* between them (i.e., *that which* brings about the differentiation of these two things in the first place). A gap has boundaries and thus a form, however

primitive; it is not indefinite, much less an endless and empty, space.[1]

The relationship between openness and an emergent order is one of many things explored in a recent book, *Closure* (2001), by the British philosopher Hilary Lawson. By 'closure', Lawson refers to the process by which meanings, ideas or objects come to be formed out of 'openness', that is, infinite, indistinguishable, undifferentiated potential (although to define openness in even such vague terms is to subject it to closure also). Closure is a form of fixing that which was previously in flux, no matter how provisionally, of making actual that which was previously the merely possible. Or as he remarks: 'It is through closure that openness is divided into things.' He goes on:

> Closure enables us to realise objects of every type and variety. Closure is responsible for our being able to describe the atoms of hydrogen and the molecules of water that make up the sea; for our being able to experience a sunrise over a field of corn; or hear the sound of a log fire and the warmth that it brings; it is closure that makes possible the kiss of a lover or the pain of injury; closure that allows the crossword puzzle and its solution; the words of language and the meanings they offer; Newton's theory of gravity and Shakespeare's sonnets; the state of peace and the activity of war; a society based on democracy; the universe; its beginning and its end. Without closure there would be no thing.[2]

It is not difficult, then, for us to consider both openness and chaos as related concepts, as that from which all things become possible. It is true that in both we find not acts of creation from nothing — *ex nihilo nihil fit*, as the medieval dictum had it, from nothing nothing can be made — but rather a process of increasing differentiation, a movement from the less to the more determinate. While none of us can lay claim to an act of primal creation — at the very least, we're in the wrong place at the wrong time — we are all constantly performing acts of closure (indeed, we are ourselves forms of closure determined by innumerable acts which go back to that originating creation). Of course these acts can be many and varied, and can have many different types of consequences, from the localised to the global (indeed, the smaller can accumulate until it becomes the larger) but the very fact of their generating a consequence means that these acts of closure are themselves forms of openness upon which further closures can be enacted. The fact that a further closure can be made means that despite how much it is sought by some — we increasingly hear of a desire 'to achieve closure' with regard to some issue or other — it is openness that persists.

Such openness is more welcome in some areas of activity than others, and I would suggest that it is in art that it is most welcome of all. Art is a form of closure that most often attempts to engage with openness, to encourage openness, and this is especially true in the art of Mike Nelson. It is not that closure is abandoned — on the contrary, Nelson's work often consists of an overwhelming multitude of materials, constructions, acts and gestures — but rather that it is postponed, or delayed as Duchamp might have had it. At times we might find his installations baffling but then, particularly if we consider a work such as *The Coral Reef* (2000) — an enormous labyrinth of rooms and corridors which seem to shift their relative positions as one walks through them — they are often constructed like a series of baffles, devices used to impede or control, with the caveat that here their conceptual force is amplified rather than muffled. Perhaps I might be excused another act of literal-mindedness here, and that is in Nelson's use of doorways. Of course a door may be open or closed (or in the case of the one fitted by Duchamp between three rooms, both open and closed at the same time); it might also be neither of these things and, as the riddle has it, no longer even a door, when it is ajar. In such a state, however, it can prevent our passage while simultaneously allowing us to catch a glimpse of where we might otherwise go, and there seems something strangely transformational in this (even the door becomes something else). It is not just the doors that are intermediate areas, however, but often also the rooms of which they are a part. Indeed, Nelson's rooms are often less rooms than anterooms, places in which we might wait, or pass through, but seldom dwell. This is true of the cinema foyer in this new installation, as it is of a number of earlier works, although to describe any of these as transitory areas would be inaccurate. Instead, we might be better served by following Casey's adoption of D.W. Winnicott's notion of 'transitional space', and

in terms that are interesting to consider with regards to the cinema foyer, Casey remarks that:

> Just as the child in transitional space exists between harsh external reality and self-serving internal fantasy, so the person on the porch — or in other comparable intermediate places — exists between private and public or between the rigors of the journey and the comforts of habitation. Instead of being merely transitory, i.e., a superficial way station, a truly transitional space is often a place for creative action, providing enough protection to encourage experimentation (if not outright exploration) without being overly confusing.[3]

The cinema foyer is a particularly complex form of transitional space, then, in that it acts as a third area between the world of external reality and an interior world of fantasy, as represented by cinema itself, the sole domain of neither but shared by both. Just as in the paradox of the door that is both open and closed, the transitional space allows for seemingly opposing elements to be maintained without any form of simplistic resolution in synthesis. In order that we might fully engage in such a situation, a situation such as that presented by Nelson, we must find ourselves in a space that is dominated by neither world, neither external reality nor interior fantasy, but in the third space which opens onto both. To find ourselves too closely aligned to either would suggest that we have been denied the opportunity for creativity, of *play* — an important concept for Winnicott — and in doing so lessens our engagement with both.

This relationship between external reality and interior fantasy is most clearly dramatised as we move beyond the cinema foyer — a space at once completely convincing and yet obviously false — into another part of the installation. Here Nelson has recreated the front room of a Victorian London terraced house, actually his former home in south London, in which the living room was transformed into the artist's studio, itself a form of transitional space. Peering inside we can see piled high the reassuring objects of artistic production (reassuring to those familiar with a practice such as Nelson's at least) — an old stereo, some thrift-store paintings, discarded packaging from books by Marx and Engels, and a number of decapitated Virgin Marys. Nelson has recreated his workspace before, or rather reimagined it as an Alchemist's desk, in his 1998 work *The Black Art Barbecue, San Antonio, August 1961*, the title taken from four drawings found within the work itself. Nelson based the reimagining of his workspace on an engraving by Albrecht Dürer entitled *Saint Jerome in his Study* (1514), and of course it is a commonplace to consider the artist's practice as in some sense comparable to that of the alchemist, with both engaged in an exploratory process of transforming base material into something of far greater value (however we might define that value, whether monetary, spiritual or intellectual). In this new installation, the studio becomes a projection room, the bay window becoming a frame through which to view a video that Nelson bought in a market in San Francisco. The video itself is cheaply produced and features a middle-aged man in glasses, a tie-mike attached to his striped shirt, who appears to be giving an illustrated lecture. If we are fortunate to have caught the beginning of the video an onscreen title confirms that this is, indeed, the case: 'Jordan Maxwell — "Basic Slide Presentation," January 30, 1993, Arcadia, California'. Despite the location of Maxwell's talk, however, we sense that he does not believe himself to be in a rural paradise. He begins:

> It is my contention that this is not happening by chance. I believe that these things are happening purposely, and I think that the Government is allowing these things to happen, and in many cases causing them to happen purposely according to a plan.

As in the primal scenes of creation, we seem to have come in at not quite the beginning. It soon becomes clear that 'these things [which] are happening' are part of a general breakdown of civil society — crime, gangland killings, violence, rioting — which the Government is promoting in order to instil fear into its citizens. 'They want as much chaos in society as possible' he says, but this is not the open creative space imagined in the early creation myths, but rather an emerging order of a very different type, a fascistic order in which the population become their own gaolers. It is an extreme form of the concerns raised more recently by civil liberties groups in America and Europe, particularly following the events on 11 September 2001 and the subsequent introduction of authoritarian measures necessary, it is claimed, to preserve our freedom. Of course, in Maxwell's view it is not simply the Government responsible for such actions, but a whole network of secret societies consisting of the Illuminati — a secret society from Bavaria whose symbol appears on the dollar bill — as well as the Knights Templar, Knights of Malta, and other Masonic organisations. (It has been Maxwell's self-appointed task over decades now to expose the reality of the Elite's control — his personal website announces that it is part of the 'Truthseeker Network' — and so the description of him in a recent interview as the 'Godfather of Secret Societies' is a cruel irony.)

Throughout his presentation, Maxwell shows a vast number of slides in which the geometric symbols of the Elite can be seen in the mass of imagery that surrounds us, whether it be the conjoined Xs in the Exxon logo which becomes the Double Cross of eastern freemasonry, or the Shell logo, which is revealed, instead, as a sun rising between mountains and thereby signifying a new world order. (Interestingly, Maxwell claims that when he writes to these companies, pointing out this symbolism hidden in full view, they respond in the affirmative and confirm his accusations, although unfortunately he didn't bring these letters with him to the presentation and didn't think to include them amongst the mass of far less damning material he has copied onto slide. He also claims to have a photograph of all the living ex-Presidents of the United States wearing red and black KKK robes and standing before a pit of fire, a twenty-foot owl symbol behind them.) 'These people are causing, financing, organising, directing chaos, and for what purpose? To bring about a new order,' he asserts, while pointing to a number of pieces of Masonic literature which carry the proclamation, 'Ordo Ab Chao', order out of chaos. Quite what this order might be, or how the power of the Elite could be increased given that they appear to control all the major world governments, banks, corporations, as well as the United Nations, is never made entirely clear, which is unfortunate, although Maxwell implores us to open our eyes and see what is plain to see all around us, that 'we're being had'. Maxwell's close scrutiny of the symbols of power may be the result of a more selfish motivation, however: in January 2003 the Federal Trade Commission announced that through one of his companies, Better Books and Cassettes of America, Maxwell was selling fake International Driver's Permits over the internet at a cost of $85 each, whereas the real permits, available only from the American Automobile Association and the American Automobile Touring Alliance, cost only $10. As Maxwell correctly attributes to Abraham Lincoln, but otherwise misquotes: 'You can fool some of the people some of the time, and most of the people all of the time, but you can't fool everybody, all the time…' It is another cruel irony for Maxwell that it is no longer Lincoln that is best remembered for saying these lines but P.T. Barnum, the well-known showman and fraud.

While one would obviously be wise to meet Maxwell's scepticism with a greater scepticism of one's own, it is perhaps worthwhile taking note of his remarks on the importance of geometry in the workings of power, and to those who are said to possess it (Masonic symbolism abounds with the geometer's tools, such as compasses and squares, for example). Geometric forms have long played an important part in Mike Nelson's work also, whether the intricate Islamic pattern cast in concrete upon the floor of an abandoned barn in Yorkshire in 1991 or, similarly, the 'Koranic kufic script taken from the prayer hall of the Khulfala Mosque, Baghdad built by the architect M. Makiya in 1960–63' and cast in concrete in the grounds of The Economist building in central London in 1993 (we might also recall the photograph used upon the private view invitation for Nelson's 1996 exhibition in Bucharest where the artist can be seen, squatting, stick in hand, while attempting to teach a bemused Romanian dog the basic Platonic forms of triangle, circle and square). Once we begin to think along these lines, we might even recall the octagonal shape of the constructed cinema foyer and wonder whether it is intentional that this transitional space shares its form with the baptismal font (it was eight days after entering Jerusalem that Jesus rose from the grave).

In his 1967 book, *Secrets of Ancient Geometry - and Its Use*, the Danish writer Tons Brunes claims that the octagon formed by the process known as the 'Sacred Cut' forms the basis for a system of geometry which has governed the construction of monuments from the time of the Ancient Egyptians. It is perhaps somewhat surprising to discover that the American artist Robert Smithson did not own a copy of this work, given his voracious bibliophilia and immense interest in the subject (at the time of his premature death in 1973 he owned 100 books on mythology and religion, with many more on science, technology and philosophy). Smithson was well aware of the importance of geometric form in the practice of a number of his contemporaries such as Don Judd and Sol LeWitt, Ronald Bladen and Peter Hutchinson, as well as within his own practice, and considered their work in a couple of early pieces of writing, such as 'Entropy and the New Monuments' published in *Artforum* in June, 1966, or 'The X Factor in Art' which appeared in *Harper's Bazaar* the following month. Here, alongside contributions from Robert Morris and Ad Reinhardt, Smithson wrote:

> The artist embodies in his work not only the facts of addition, subtraction, multiplication and division, but also the structure of the numbers system in terms of modules and units. Concepts such as mathematical crystal structure, set theory, clock math, and the Cuisenaire rod method, disclose to the new artist uncharted, abstract territories of the mind that he explores in terms of concrete structure.[4]

Smithson's interest was not in the purity of static form, however, but in what might be termed dynamic geometry, the often slow but undeniable developing structures of crystalline growth or geological formation in which was made visible the 'shape of time', to borrow the title of a book by George Kubler which was particularly influential fo the artist. In acknowledging the importance of the growth of structures over time, Smithson became increasingly engaged with their disintegration also, and over the next few years it was the process of entropy which would assume growing importance within his extraordinary practice. This can perhaps be most clearly seen in *Partially Buried Woodshed*, a work the artist made early in 1970, on the campus of Kent State University and which has now been adopted by Nelson in the final part of his installation in Oxford.

Smithson was brought to Kent State by his friend Robert Swick, a student there at the time, in order to give a public lecture, take student critiques and then make a piece of work. It turned out to be one of the most severe winters on record — Smithson caught flu — and the cold which slowed down Smithson had already brought his proposed work to a complete stop: a mud flow work which he had proposed a number of times already, although it was yet to be realised. (In fact, Hans Haacke *had* already realised a similar project in Seattle the previous year, where a sprinkler system flooded an area of lawn, eroding the soil and turning the area into a pool of mud.) That same January week, another of Smithson's flow works, *Glue Pour*, was made in Vancouver as part of Lucy Lippard's exhibition *955,000* (the population of the city) in which a barrel of thick, orange, industrial glue made its heavy way down a slope of soil and gravel, sticking to itself and the earth across which it travelled, picking up debris as it stumbled uncertainly down. But flow the glue did, no matter how slowly; in the frozen north east of Ohio mud would not.

Smithson retreated to the home of sculpture professor Brinsley Tyrrell, and began to make his arrangements to return home. The students, with whom he had been working all week, would not let him leave however, visiting him at Tyrrell's home and asking him what else they could do. Smithson said he had always liked the idea of burying a building, and so work began on the project. The building chosen was a partially-derelict woodshed, part of an abandoned farm located on a back lot of the university campus, and now used to store dirt, gravel and firewood. And so on 22 January 1970, with students looking on and some filming the event on super-8, local building contractor Rich Hemling sat upon his Allis Chalmers D15 tractor as though riding some jerky mechanical dinosaur and, under the direction of the shivering artist, proceeded to backhoe twenty truckloads of dirt from a campus construction site onto the shed until its central beam cracked. The artist then signed a document donating the work and a forty-five-foot area surrounding it to the University, although Smithson insisted that it was to be accepted as a permanent work and, while natural alterations and weathering was considered part of the work, there was to be no other form of alteration or removal. Three-and-a-half years after writing 'Entropy and the New Monuments', Smithson had created a Monument to Entropy.

This monumental aspect of the work was to be made even more explicit in the months to come. On 23 January 1970, the student newspaper, the *Daily Kent Stater*, published a photograph of the *Partially Buried Woodshed* with a brief caption on its front page, although much of the paper consisted of articles relating to the increased tensions between students and university law enforcement agencies following the American invasion of Cambodia. In terms which might be reminiscent of — although perhaps at odds with — Jordan Maxwell's comments on the execution of control in times of uncertainty, an article on the Law Enforcement Administration Program remarks that, 'Although much of our social control has broken down, tougher harder and more stringent punishment is not the answer. In a society that is attacking the basic roots and causes of disorder, the answer can only be enlightened law enforcement.' This was not the answer given by the National Guard a few months later, however; on 4 May 1970, during another campus protest, they opened fire on groups of students — some of whom were not even participating in the protests — killing four and wounding nine others. The campus was closed and the incident became widely reported both nationally and internationally; nobody was ever brought to justice for the killings.

For many, the shootings marked a rupture in a disintegrating political structure, a point of no return, just like the breaking of the central beam in the woodshed. As the artist Nancy Holt, Smithson's widow, later recalled:

> I think one of the most shocking things, when I look back, were the Kent shootings. It shocked me more than the president getting assassinated. I think it changed everyone's mind, even those who were conservative. So many people just switched overnight after that. Everything just became very, very clear. [5]

Earlier, in a letter from 1975, Holt wrote that she believed the *Partially Buried Woodshed* to be 'intrinsically political', and that Smithson himself had seen it as 'prophetic'. The connection between the work and the shootings was made even more explicit when, sometime during the summer while the campus was closed, someone painted in bold white letters on the structure: 'MAY 4 KENT 70'. As Holt later commented:

> Obviously the students, or whoever did that graffiti — it's an example of graffiti that enhances — the students obviously recognised the parallel. Piling the earth until the central beam cracked, as though the whole government, the whole country were cracking. Really, we had a revolution then. It was the end of one society and the beginning of the next.[6]

In reimagining the *Woodshed* in a desert environment, as though emerging from shifting sands, Nelson not only emphasises the work's status as a monument — much as Smithson emphasised everyday monuments in works such as 'A Tour of the Monuments of Passaic, New Jersey' (1967) — but also its relationship to tropes within contemporary science fiction, a genre in which Smithson was especially interested. Of course, it is especially important in the context of this publication that we acknowledge that the term 'Earthwork' which was used to describe works by Smithson, Michael Heizer and others was taken by Smithson from a dystopian science fiction novel of the same name by Brian Aldiss, published in 1965, and used by Smithson in October 1968 as the title for an exhibition at the Dwan Gallery, New York, of such works by fourteen artists (Smithson describes buying his copy of the book at the Port Authority Building in New York on 20 September 1967, a paperback published by Signet just two months previously, just before buying his bus ticket for 'Tour of the Monuments of Passaic'). As Smithson was well aware, science fiction provides a means of social or political comment which might otherwise be too difficult to make, or which might fall foul of the authorities (think of its importance to the dissident tradition in the Soviet Union and other authoritarian states) and this is apparent not only in his *Woodshed*, but in Nelson's installation also, itself an oblique but no less angry confrontation with the barren nature of much contemporary political thinking, and the resultant desolation that is visited upon entire peoples. We might recall the climatic scene in *Planet of the Apes* (1968) for example, when Charlton Heston's astronaut character Taylor discovers the Statue of Liberty, partially-buried, and realises that the planet on which he had crash-landed was none other than the earth, the apes' dominance of the earth a form of evolutionary reversal following nuclear catastrophe: 'You maniacs! You blew it up! Damn you! God damn you all to hell!'

Not only has the *Woodshed* been described using a term taken from science fiction, but I would suggest that it — and Nelson's reimagining — acts in a comparable way, that they too might be considered as examples of science fiction. Nelson points to J.G. Ballard's *The Crystal World* (1966), with its increasingly crystalline landscape as an important point of reference here, as I think it must have been for Smithson himself (perhaps coincidently, in May that year *Harper's Bazaar* published an article by Smithson called 'The Crystal Land', a reflection upon a rock hunting excursion in New Jersey with Don Judd); I am reminded more of an earlier Ballard story, 'The Time Tombs', published in the science fiction magazine *If* in March 1963, in which a group of tomb-robbers pillage some of the estimated twenty-thousand tombs buried beneath restless sands in order to lay claim upon the memory tapes that are contained within, 'three-dimensional molecular transcriptions of their living originals, stored among the dunes as a stupendous act of faith, in the hope that one day the physical re-creation of the coded personalities would be possible.' When the tombs are entered, the contents of the tapes are projected into the space, a relaying of life as representation, and it is with one of the visions of a woman that the central character, Shepley, becomes increasingly obsessed. He is caught by the time-wardens who patrol the area in order to safe-guard the tombs as he watches the image slowly disintegrate, aware of the unusual nature of the tomb as one in which the person portrayed was already dead at the point of their encoding. One of the robbers comments that such tombs were sometimes left intact — 'giving immortality only to the dead' — and in a sense this is what Nelson has done here also, resurrecting a work which was created through an act of disintegration and which was finally destroyed fourteen years later. As Ballard was later to write on the importance of cataclysms to science fiction:

> I believe that the catastrophe story, whoever may tell it, represents a constructive and positive act by the imagination rather than a negative one, an attempt to confront the terrifying void of a patently meaningless universe by challenging it at its own game, to remake zero by provoking it in every conceivable way. [7]

In describing one of the motivations of his own practice Ballard, with typical perspicuity, might be seen to illuminate those of Smithson and Nelson also. Like Ballard and Smithson, like the writer of science fiction, or of the creation myths with which we also began so long ago, Nelson has created a space of immense creative possibilities, a chaotic space, within which points of order — emotional and intellectual — are able to emerge.

1 Edward S. Casey, *The Fate of Place - A Philosophical History*, University of California Press, Berkeley, Los Angeles and London, 1998, p.9

2 Hilary Lawson, *Closure - A Story of Everything*, Routledge, London, 2001, p.165

3 Edward S. Casey, *Getting Back into Place - Towards a Renewed Understanding of the Place-World*, Indiana University Press, Bloomington and Indianapolis, 1993, pp.121–2

4 Robert Smithson, 'The X Factor in Art', *Harpar's Bazaar*, July 1966, quoted in Jack Flam (ed.), *Roberts Smithson: The Collected Writings* University of California Press, Berkeley and Los Angeles, 1996, p.25

5 Quoted in Dorothy Shinn, *Robert Smithson's partially Buried Woodshed*, Kent State University Art Gallery, Kent State, 1990, n.p.

6 Ibid.

7 J.G. Ballard, 'Cataclysms and Dooms', in Brian Ash (ed.), *The Visual Encyclopedia of Science Fiction*, Pan Books, London and Sydney, 1977, p.130

PLEASE MIND YOUR HEAD